"If you do not train in technique, but only fill your breast with principle,
you and your hands will not function."
- Takuan Soho

Copyright © Michael Jacyna

All rights reserved. No part of this publication may be reproduced or used in any way or means, electronic or mechanical, including photocopying and recording without prior written permission from the author.

For further information on this and other aikido related books visit:
ExploreAikido.com

ISBN-13: 978-1948038010

Library of Congress Control Number: 2017916460

Explore AIKIDO Vol. 2

Aiki-Jo Staff Techniques in Aikido

Michael Jacyna

Content

Preface 7

Aiki-jo etiquette 8

Aiki-jo forms & technical aspects 14

Aiki-jo suburi 20

Choku tsuki kihons 46

Kaeshi tsuki kihons 78

Furi komi tsuki kihons 110

Two direction kihons 142

Jo nage 176

Jo dori 204

Kumi jo 228

Glossary 253

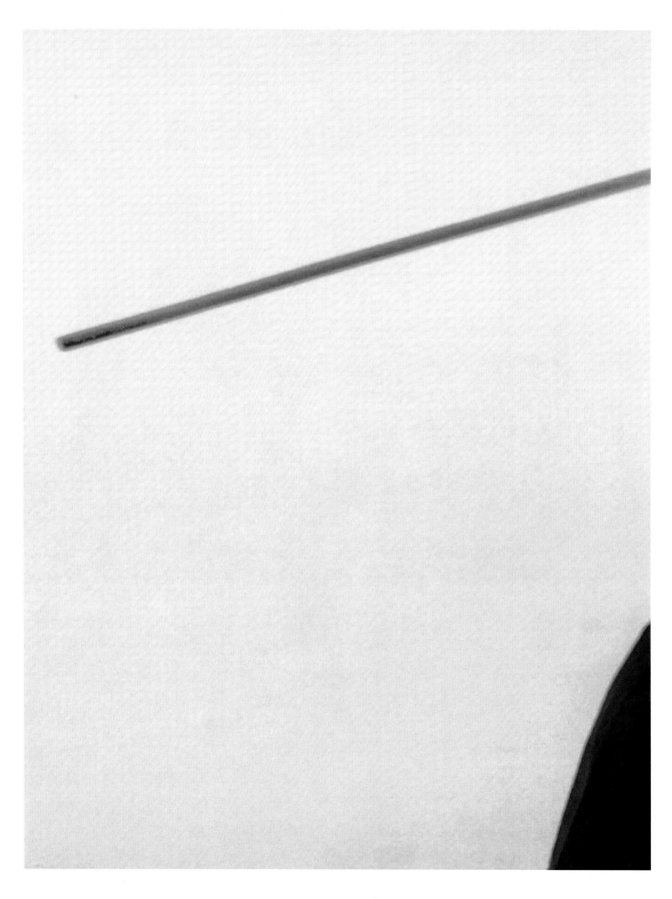

Preface

Aiki-jo is an integral part of aikido training. It plays an important role in understanding the concept of distance, timing, and body coordination.

In this volume, I strive to present aikido staff techniques from an accessible and transparent viewpoint, where the reader can observe and relate to the technical aspects of the art form. Keep in mind, however, that as transparent and visually accessible this volume may be, it is not a substitute for training in the dojo under the guidance of a qualified and knowledgeable teacher who can present, explain, and clarify the nuances of each technique.

For those who have yet to experience aikido, I hope this book will inspire and ignite your journey. For aikido enthusiasts, I hope this book will serve as a fundamental guide. As for seasoned aikidokas, I hope this book will provide you with thought provoking material.

I would like to express my gratitude and appreciation to my instructors who have influenced me both on and off the mat: Jacek Wysocki, and the late Giampietro Savegnago, thank you.

I would like to thank my students: Aaron Bush, Marie Visisombat, Zachary Nikolayev and Andrey Yevdoshchenko, for their time, effort, and dedication during the photo-shoots, and the making of this book.

Aiki-Jo Etiquette

Aiki-jo training, same as aiki-tai jutsu, begins and ends with etiquette. Implementation of etiquette within aiki-jo practice creates mutual respect among all class participants and results in an organized and safe training environment.

There are a few basic things to remember during aiki-jo etiquette. During lineup with the jo and/or during bowing, the jo should be held in the middle with the right hand. The right arm should be loose and, when standing upright, the front tip of the jo should be at the arm pit level. During tachi rei, point the front tip of the jo toward the ground and then the bow follows. On the way up, the jo and upper body simultaneously rise. After the bow, aikidokas begin aiki-jo training. During that time, all aiki-jo practice begins in hidari hanmi (left profile stance).

On the following pages are examples of bowing and transferring of the jo between teacher and student, and between peers.

Bow between teacher and student

When sensei and deshi bow to each other during aiki-jo sessions, sensei bows standing and deshi bows seated. This is implemented whenever a student is assisting the instructor during presentation and/or after receiving advice during practice (pic. 1-4).

Jo transfer between teacher and student

When transferring the jo between teacher and student, and vice versa, the standing teacher receives or presents the jo to the seated student. In the example below, the instructor transfers the jo to the student. As the jo changes hands, both the teacher and the student bow. Once the jo is transfered, the student places the jo on the right hand side (pic. 1-6).

Za rei, seated bow between peers

When students bow to each other in seiza, their jo is on the right hand side (pic. 1-5).

Tachi rei, standing bow between peers with the jo

When standing students bow to each other, they first point their jo toward the ground, and then bow. As they rise, the jo and upper body go up simultaneously.

Jo transfer between peers

When transferring the jo between peers, one student raises the jo from the right hand side to the front, and the other student takes hold of the jo. At that moment, both aikidokas bow, and the jo receiving student holds the jo on the right hand side (pic. 1-6).

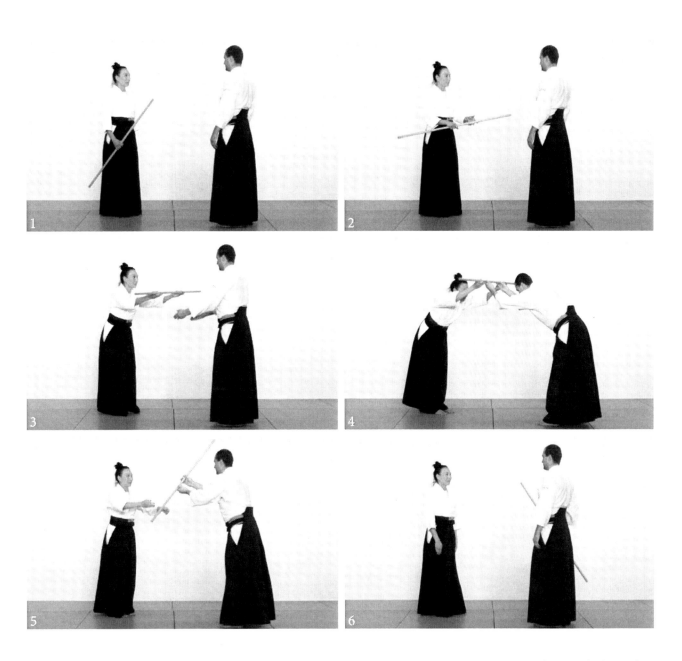

Aiki-Jo Forms & Technical Aspects

Regardless of the practitioner's height and/or size, the standard jo length is 50.25 inches or 132 cm and the jo diameter is just under 1 inch or 24mm. Note that in case of kids training, the jo sizing formula may be adjusted. A quality jo is usually made by hand from Japanese white oak. This wood choice provides the jo with great durability, excellent weight distribution, and balance.

Aiki-Jo Forms. There are five different arrangements in which aiki-jo can be practiced:

1. **Jo suburi** is a repetitive practice of singular strikes, blocks, entries, and other basic moves.
2. **Jo kihon** are forms that consist of suburi. They can be practiced alone or with a partner.
3. **Jo nage** is part of aiki-jo, where we use the jo to throw uke.
4. **Jo dori** are disarming techniques against uke equipped/attacking with the jo.
5. **Kumi jo** is an aiki-jo setup where shite (defender) and seme (attacker) are equipped with the jo.

Aiki-Jo Technical Aspects
There are few things to remember during aiki-jo training to help organize and understand the system:

1. Control one end of the jo.

It is important to control one end of the jo at all times. There are a few exceptions to that rule but in 99% of aiki-jo training this rule is applied.

View an example of choku tsuki. Aikidoka begins in left profile stance and holds the top end of the jo with his left hand. The jo stands upright on his center line. Before releasing the front end of the jo, he first takes control of the back end and then releases the front (pic. 1-3).

2. No guard at the beginning of techniques

In aiki-jo, just as in aiki-tai jutsu, there is no guard at the beginning of techniques. View the kumi jo example below. Shite and seme begin in left profile stance with the jo standing on their center line. Both control the top end of their jo (pic. 1). As seme begins to attack, shite opens up, inviting the attack. By doing so, shite creates a trap into which seme will fall (pic. 2). At the last moment, when it is too late for seme to change the direction of the attack, shite counters with furi komi tsuki (pic. 3).

3. Distance

Distance is an important element within aiki-jo. View of different aiki-jo training and the appropriate distance examples below.

Kumi Jo is part of aiki-jo training where both the defender and the attacker are equipped with the jo. Jo against jo training distance is approximately one tatami length, which equals roughly six and a half feet or two meters. In other words, it is a distance one step away, where in order to reach the partner, the other person needs to step forward (pic. 1).

Jo Nage is part of aiki-jo training where we use the jo to throw the other person. Distance in this case is also one step away, meaning uke is one step away from reaching tori's jo (pic. 2).

Jo Dori is part of aiki-jo training where we defend against the jo attack. Same as with the previous two examples, the distance is one step away, meaning the attacker is one step away from reaching the defender (pic. 3).

4. Jo extends from the center line

The jo should extend from *hara* or from one's center line. View examples below. At the end of choku tsuki, if we drew a line from one end of the jo to the other, the line would extend toward one's center line and/or toward one's obi knot (pic. 1).

The second example is kaeshi tsuki from a front view. As you can see, the jo extends toward the center and the hakama knot (pic.2)

5. Profile position

All aiki-jo, as well as aiki-tai jutsu and aiki-ken training incorporates profile position. It is an efficient and effective way of practice. By using a profile position, one minimizes the target area otherwise exposed to a possible attack.

6. Center line control

Center line control is a repetitive element throughout all aikido areas, including aiki-tai jutsu, aiki-jo, and aiki-ken. In kumi-jo, for example, instead of fighting the opponents' jo, it is more effective to control opponents' center line be it jodan, judan, or gedan level. This will put the opponent into defensive mode. When you control the center line, you control the situation.

7. Oto nashi no jo - silent jo

This is a clever, efficient concept. In a nut shell it means having the ability to avoid your partner's block by being a split of a second ahead of your partner's action. Understanding the finesse behind this idea and being able to put it into practice make aiki-jo training very effective.

8. Jo striking parts

In most cases in aiki-jo, we only use both ends of the jo and its round edges to strike with.

9. Jo striking target areas

There are a few basic striking areas in aiki-jo. Please view some of the examples below:

1. Abdomen

2. Throat/face

3. Temple

4. Knee

5. Kidney

6. Wrist

7. Ankle

8. Elbow

Aiki-Jo Suburi

Suburi training, a repetitive practice of singular strikes, blocks, entries, and other basic moves. It is a good way to develop proper technique, posture, speed, strength, and body coordination.

Aiki-jo suburi · choku tsuki - profile view

Choku tsuki is a basic forward thrust. Begin in left profile stance, holding the top end of the jo with your left hand. Bring the jo up, grab it with your right hand, and slide your hand all the way to the back end of the jo. Once you control both ends of the jo, simultaneously move forward and release the front end of the jo. At the end, the right hand holds the jo at the back end and the left hand is located between 1/4 and 1/3 of the jo length from the back end (pic. 1-6).

Choku tsuki may be performed as an attack or counter attack. See the following pages.

Aiki-jo suburi · choku tsuki - front view, seme (the attacker) on the line

This is choku tsuki as performed during an attack. Notice that seme and his jo stay on the line of the attack from the beginning to the end (pic. 1-6). This is the shortest and fastest way to reach the target.

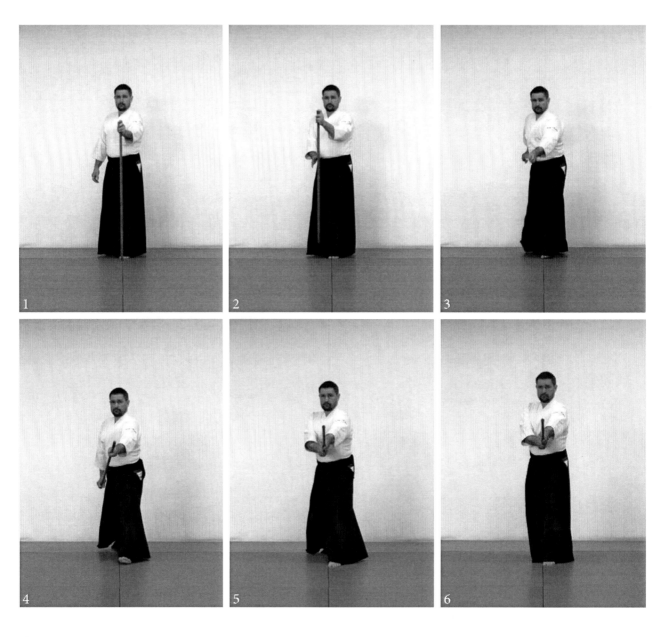

Aiki-jo suburi · choku tsuki - front view, shite (the defender) off the line.

Here you can see choku tsuki as performed by shite in a counter attack application. Notice that shite opens up his position by holding the jo sideways (pic. 1-3). This lures in the attack/attacker. Shite then moves directly toward the direction of the attack (pic. 4). At the last moment, he moves his right hip off the line and releases the jo. The front end of the jo stays on the line (pic. 5-6).

Aiki-jo suburi · choku tsuki - linear exercise

Begin with choku tsuki (pic.1). Through a vertical trajectory, while changing profile without stepping, pull the front end of the jo to the back (pic. 2-3). Change the grip on both ends of the jo (pic. 4-5). Step forward and simultaneously release the front end of the jo (pic. 6-7). Repeat the same action in the opposite profile (pic. 8-10).

Aiki-jo suburi · kaeshi tsuki - profile view

Kaeshi tsuki is a reverse strike. Begin in left profile stance, holding the top end of the jo with your left hand. Slide your left hand down and take over the top end of the jo with your right hand, thumb down (pic. 1-2). Start kaeshi tsuki on a crescent trajectory and simultaneously move forward (pic. 3-5). The strike aims at the temple height (pic. 6).

Explore Aikido Vol. 2

Aiki-jo suburi · kaeshi tsuki - front view; seme on the line

Here is kaeshi tsuki performed as an attack without stepping off the line. Begin in left profile stance, holding the top end of the jo with your left hand. Slide your left hand down and take over the top end of the jo with your right hand, thumb down (pic. 1-2). Start kaeshi tsuki on a crescent trajectory and, at the same time, move forward (pic. 3-6). The strike ends at the temple height.

Aiki-jo suburi · kaeshi tsuki - front view; shite off the line

Here you can see kaeshi tsuki performed by shite as a counter attack. Begin in left profile stance, holding the top end of the jo with your left hand. Slide your left hand down and take over the top end of the jo with your right hand, thumb down (pic. 1-2). Begin to move forward and simultaneously execute kaeshi tsuki (pic. 3-4). At the last moment, move your right hip off the line (pic. 5-6).

Aiki-jo suburi · kaeshi tsuki - linear exercise

Begin with kaeshi tsuki strike (pic. 1). Retract the front end of the jo without moving your front hand back (pic. 2). Release the back end of the jo and execute kaeshi tsuki in a vertical circular trajectory, while simultaneously stepping forward (pic. 3-4). Continue the same move in the opposite profile (pic. 5-7). Note that during kaeshi tsuki linear exercise your hands do not change or regrab the jo. They stay in the same hold and simply slide along the jo.

Aiki-jo suburi · furi komi tsuki - profile view

Furi komi tsuki is a thrust coming from the bottom up. Begin in left profile stance holding the top of the jo with your left hand. Slide your left hand down and take over the top of the jo with your right hand. Use your right thumb to cap the top of the jo (pic. 1-2). Move forward and simultaneously begin furi komi tsuki by lifting off the ground the bottom of the jo and bringing the top hold of the jo under your left collar bone (pic. 3-5). The target for furi komi tsuki is jodan, which includes neck and face. At the end of furi komi tsuki, your front arm extends and wraps around the jo with thumb on top. Your right arm and elbow are close to your body (pic. 6).

Aiki-jo suburi · furi komi tsuki - front view, seme on the line

Furi komi tsuki as performed by the attacker. The execution is the same as on the previous page. Note, in this case, aikidoka does not move off the line and executes the strike directly on the line (pic. 1-6).

Explore Aikido Vol. 2

Aiki-jo suburi · furi komi tsuki - front view, shite off the line

Here is an example of furi komi tsuki performed off the line. Begin in left profile stance and hold the top end of the jo. Slide your left hand down and cap the top of the jo with your right hand (pic. 1-2). Move forward and release furi komi tsuki (pic. 3-4). At the last moment, move your back hip off the line (pic. 5-6).

Aiki-jo suburi · furi komi tsuki - linear exercise

Begin in furi komi tsuki position (pic. 1). Retract and bring the jo horizontally downward (pic. 2-3). Change your grip on both ends (pic. 4). Release the back end of the jo, step forward, and execute furi komi tsuki (pic. 5-7). Repeat the same action on the other side (pic. 8-9).

Aiki-jo suburi · Shomen uchi - profile view

Shomen uchi is a vertical strike coming from the top down. Begin in left profile stance with your right hand holding the jo on the bottom and your left hand placed above your right, between 1/4 and 1/3 of the jo length. Lift the jo above your head (pic. 1-3). Release the jo on a vertical trajectory and simultaneously move forward (pic. 4-5). Shomen uchi should end at jodan level.

Note: in aiki-jo, shomen uchi can be performed in left and right profile stance. Hand placement changes depending on which profile we begin the strike in.

Aiki-jo suburi · shomen uchi - front view; seme on the line

Here you can see the front view of the same shomen uchi execution as on the previous page (pic. 1-5).

Aiki-jo suburi · shomen uchi - front view; shite off the line

This is off the line shomen uchi, usually applied during counter attack. Begin in left profile stance. Lift the jo above your head, release shomen uchi, and simultaneously move forward (pic. 1-3). At the last moment, move off the line while keeping the front end of the jo on the line (pic. 4-5).

Aiki-jo suburi · shomen uchi - linear exercise

Begin in right profile stance. While holding the bottom of the jo with your left hand and your right hand holding 1/4 to 1/3 of the jo length away, retract the jo back (pic. 1-2). Change your grip on both ends of the jo and raise the jo above your head (pic. 3). From this position, slide the jo through your left hand grip, step forward, and execute shomen uchi (pic. 4-5). Repeat the action on the opposite side (pic. 6-8).

Note: during linear jo exercises, footwork should be done on one straight line. Overall, the jo should not deviate off the line.

Uke nagashi is an absorbing/deflecting maneuver usually followed by an immediate or slightly delayed strike or thrust. There are a few basic uke nagashi variations.

Aiki-jo suburi · ue no uke nagashi - itta no maai (regular distance) - profile view

The first uke nagashi is Ue, which means "up" or "above". Begin in a choku tsuki judan position. Start to move back and sideways, off the line, while using your right hand to bring the jo above your forehead. With left hand grip, move the front end of the jo in a spiral (pic. 1-3). After ue no uke nagashi, there is a kaeshi strike that follows (pic. 4-6).

Aiki-jo suburi · shita no uke nagashi - itta no maai (regular distance) - profile view

Second uke nagashi is Shita, which means "below" or "under". Begin in a choku tsuki judan position. Lower the front end of the jo and simultaneously step forward (pic. 1-3). About half way through the step, bring the front end of the jo up to follow with tsuki jodan and zanshin (pic. 4-5).

Aiki-jo suburi · ue no uke nagashi - toma (long distance) - profile view

This uke nagashi is in long distance and it is Ue, upper. Begin in toma katate uchi position (pic. 1). Bring your right hand above your forehead and simultaneously, with the front end of the jo, create a circular trajectory (pic. 1-3). Ue no uke nagashi, in this case, turns immediately into kaeshi (pic. 4-6).

Aiki-jo suburi · shita no uke nagashi - toma (long distance) - profile view

This uke nagashi in long distance is Shita, lower. Begin in toma katate uchi position (pic. 1). Lower the jo and it's front end below judan level (pic. 2-3). After shita no uke nagashi, resurface with tsuki jodan and jodan control, while simultaneously stepping forward and adding your left hand hold to the jo (pic. 4-6).

Aiki-jo suburi · "tsuki" no uke nagashi - profile view

This is not a typical uke nagashi, but it may be included on the outskirts of that group. Begin in choku tsuki judan position (pic. 1). With your right hand, retract the jo all the way back, so that each hand controls one end of the jo. During the retraction, the front hand should stay in place (pic. 2). Release the jo and step forward (pic. 3-5). The final choku tsuki and zanshin position are jodan (pic. 6).

Aiki-jo suburi · "furi komi" no uke nagashi - **profile view**

This uke nagashi is rather atypical, as well. Begin in furi komi tsuki position (pic. 1). Move the front end of the jo downward and rotate it in a circular trajectory to return with kaeshi strike. Throughout this maneuver, simultaneously step forward (pic. 2-5). The final position of the kaeshi strike is jodan aimed at the temple or nasal bridge (pic. 6).

Aiki-jo suburi · hasso gaeshi - profile view

Hasso gaeshi is a vertical rotational strike. Depending on the kihon performed, it is applicable against one or two opponents. Begin in furi komi tsuki position (pic. 1). Turn the jo horizontally downward (pic. 2). Slide your right hand less than 1/3 of the jo length, while your left hand slides down, pushes downward, and sends the jo into vertical rotation (pic. 3-5).

As the jo rotates to an almost vertical position, use your left hand to take control of the bottom end of the jo (pic. 6). Hasso gaeshi ends in hasso no kamae, with one hand holding the jo at the chest level and the other hand holding it at the head level (pic. 7).

Choku Tsuki Kihons

Aiki-jo kihons · choku tsuki - base kihon

This choku tsuki kihon is a base or a primary kihon, without a number. There are fifteen choku tsuki kihons that follow.

Begin in left profile stance (pic. 1). Execute choku tsuki judan off the line (pic. 2-4). Slightly raise the jo and strike at the wrist level (pic. 5-6). Move forward and finish with tsuki and zanshin (pic. 7-8).

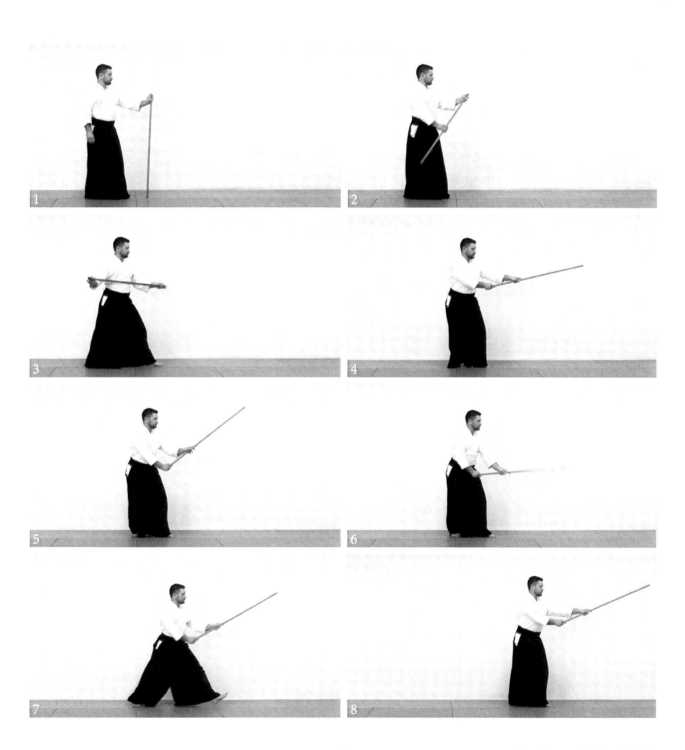

Aiki-jo kihons · choku tsuki - kihon #1

Begin in left profile stance. Execute choku tsuki judan off the line (pic. 1-4). Follow with ue no uke nagashi (pic. 5-6). Continue with tsuki jodan in full extension, then retract into ue no uke nagashi, and follow with kaeshi (pic. 7-11). Finish with another ue no uke nagashi and kaeshi (pic. 12-16).

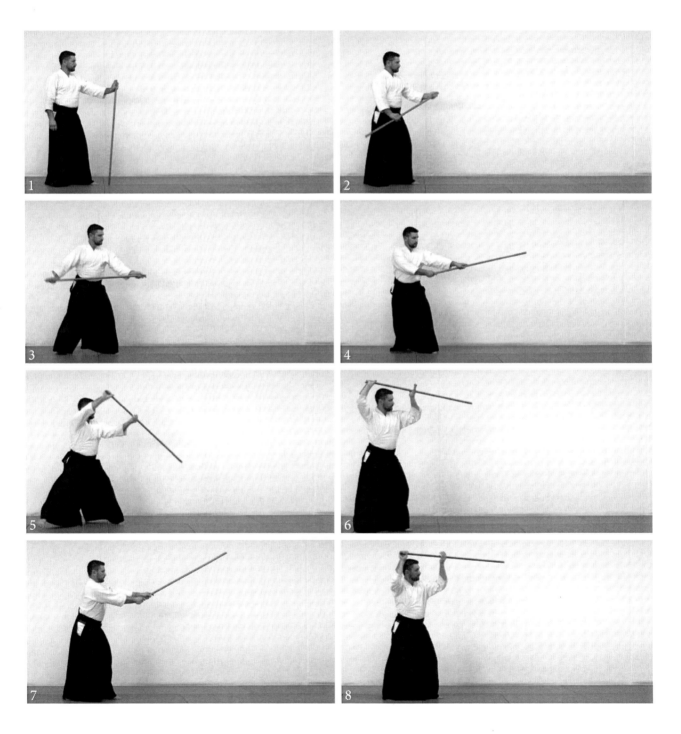

Aiki-jo kihons · choku tsuki - kihon #2

Begin in left profile stance, then execute choku tsuki judan off the line (pic. 1-4). Continue with ue no uke nagashi (pic. 5-6). Follow with tsuki jodan, shita no uke nagashi, and immediate tsuki jodan (pic. 7-10). Finish with ue no uke nagashi and kaeshi (pic. 11-14).

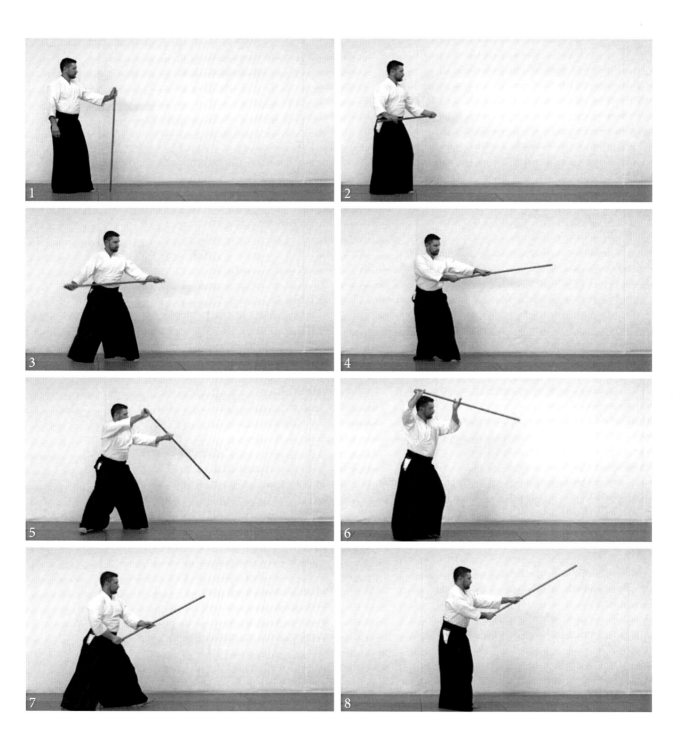

Explore Aikido Vol. 2

Aiki-jo kihons · choku tsuki - kihon #3

Begin in left profile stance. Execute choku tsuki off the line (pic. 1-4). Continue with shita no uke nagashi and tsuki jodan (pic. 5-6). Again, shita no uke nagashi and tsuki jodan with zanshin (pic. 7-9).

Aiki-jo kihons · choku tsuki - kihon #4

Begin in left profile stance. Execute choku tsuki judan off the line (pic. 1-4). Continue with ue no uke nagashi (pic. 5-6). With a slight delay, move forward with tsuki jodan (pic. 7-8). Finish with shita no uke nagashi and tsuki jodan with zanshin (pic. 9-10).

Explore Aikido Vol. 2

Aiki-jo kihons · choku tsuki - kihon #5

Begin in left profile stance. Execute choku tsuki judan off the line (pic. 1-3). Continue with ue no uke nagashi with a pull back (pic. 4-6). Finish with toma katate uchi (pic. 7-10).

Aiki-jo kihons · choku tsuki - kihon #6

Begin in left profile stance, holding the jo in the right hand at approximately 1/4-1/3 of the jo length (pic. 1). Execute tsuki jodan (pic. 2-3). Continue with ue no uke nagashi and finish with kaeshi and zanshin (pic. 4-8).

Aiki-jo kihons · choku tsuki - kihon #7

Begin in left profile stance, holding the jo in your right hand at approximately 1/4-1/3 of the jo length (pic. 1). Execute tsuki coming from the bottom up on a circular trajectory (pic. 2-4). Transition into ue no uke nagashi and finish with kaeshi and zanshin (pic. 5-8).

Aiki-jo kihons · choku tsuki - kihon #8

Begin in left profile stance. Execute choku tsuki judan off the line (pic. 1-4). Continue with tsuki no uke nagashi (pic. 5-6). Immediately return and finish with choku tsuki jodan and zanshin (pic. 7-10).

Aiki-jo kihons · choku tsuki - kihon #9

Begin in left profile stance. Execute choku tsuki judan off the line (pic. 1-4). Continue with tsuki no uke nagashi (pic. 5-6). Immediately return with kaeshi tsuki on a vertical trajectory, and zanshin (pic. 7-10).

Aiki-jo kihons · choku tsuki - kihon #10

Begin in left profile stance. Execute choku tsuki judan off the line (pic. 1-3). Continue with tsuki no uke nagashi and furi komi tsuki (pic. 4-7). Redirect the jo inward (pic. 8-9). Finish with tsuki jodan and zanshin (pic. 10-12).

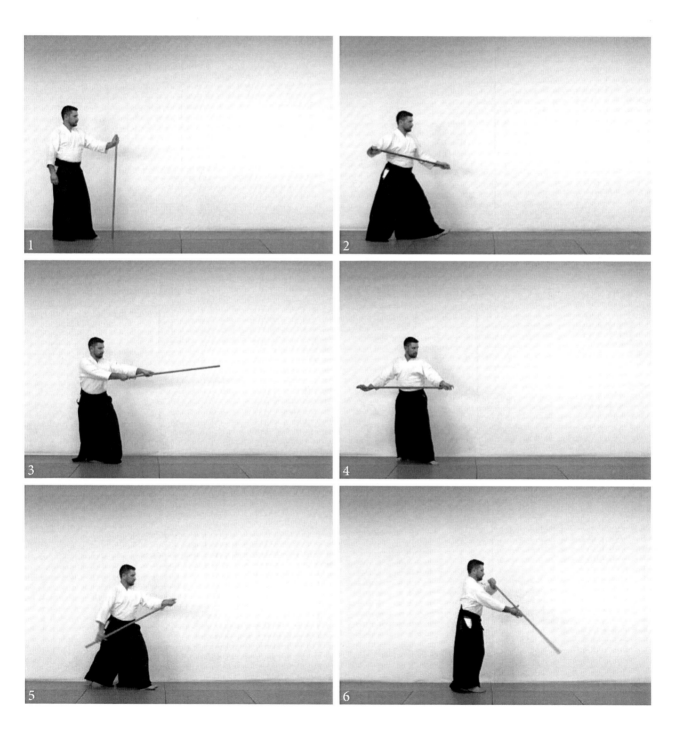

Aiki-jo kihons · choku tsuki - kihon #11

Begin in left profile stance. Execute choku tsuki judan off the line (pic. 1-4). Continue with tsuki no uke nagashi and return with choku tsuki (pic. 5-7). Then continue with another tsuki no uke nagashi and choku tsuki with zanshin (pic. 8-12).

Aiki-jo kihons · choku tsuki - kihon #12

Begin in left profile stance. Execute choku tsuki judan off the line (pic. 1-3). Continue with tsuki no uke nagashi and kaeshi gedan (pic. 4-6). Redirect the jo to judan level and finish with tsuki jodan and zanshin (pic. 7-10).

Aiki-jo kihons · choku tsuki - kihon #13

Begin in left profile stance. Execute choku tsuki judan off the line (pic. 1-3). Continue with ue no uke nagashi with a pull back (pic. 4-5). Follow with toma katate uchi, initially at jodan, then gedan level (pic. 6-9). Finish with kaeshi and zanshin (pic. 10-13).

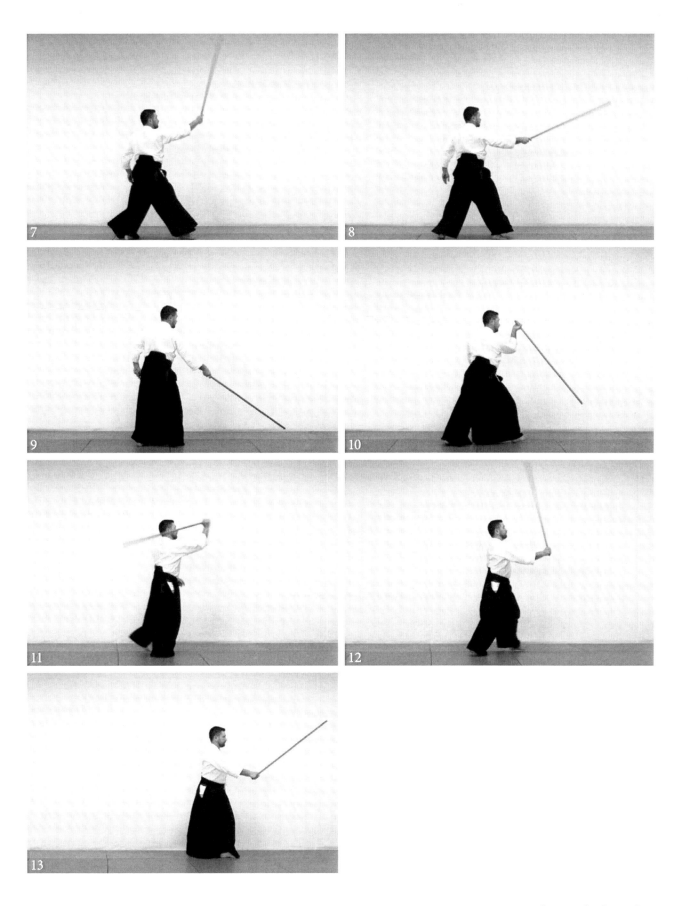

Aiki-jo kihons · choku tsuki - kihon #14

Begin in left profile stance. Execute choku tsuki judan off the line (pic. 1-4). Continue with ue no uke nagashi with a pull back (pic. 5-6). Follow with toma katate uchi, transition into ue no uke nagashi, and finish with kaeshi and zanshin (pic. 7-12).

Aiki-jo kihons · choku tsuki - kihon #15

Begin in left profile stance. Execute choku tsuki judan off the line (pic. 1-4). Continue with ue no uke nagashi with a pull back (pic. 5-6). Follow with toma katate uchi, transition into shita no uke nagashi, and finish with tsuki jodan and zanshin (pic. 7-12).

Kaeshi Tsuki Kihons

Aiki-jo kihons · kaeshi tsuki - base kihon

This kaeshi tsuki kihon is a base, or a primary kihon, without a number. There are fifteen kaeshi tsuki kihons that follow.

Begin in left profile stance. Execute kaeshi tsuki off the line (pic. 1-4). Slightly raise the jo up and strike at the wrist level (pic. 5-6). Move forward and finish with tsuki and zanshin (pic. 7-8).

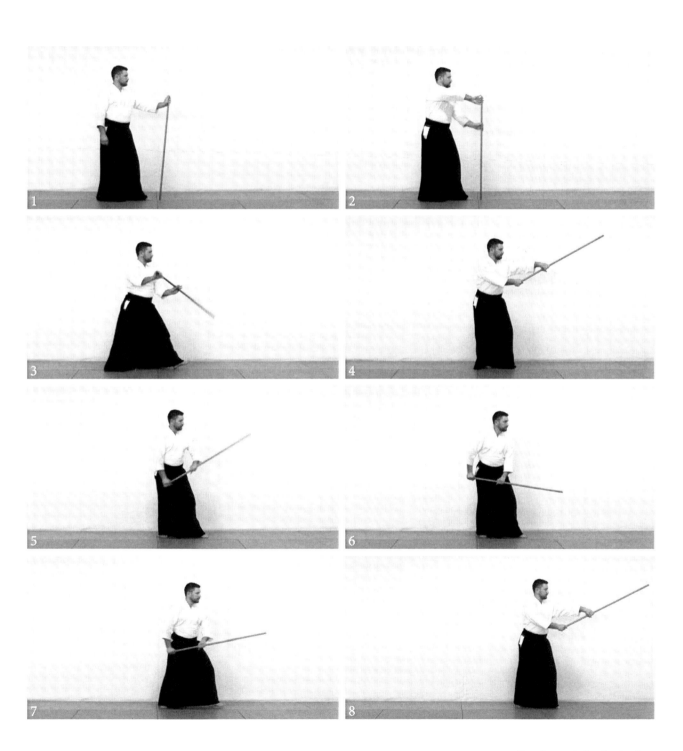

Aiki-jo kihons · kaeshi tsuki - kihon #1

Begin in left profile stance. Execute kaeshi tsuki off the line (pic. 1-4). Continue with ue no uke nagashi with a pull back (pic. 5-7). Step forward and finish with toma katate uchi and zanshin (pic. 8-12).

Aiki-jo kihons · kaeshi tsuki - kihon #2

Begin in left profile stance. Execute kaeshi tsuki off the line (pic. 1-4). Continue with ue no uke nagashi with a pull back (pic. 5-7). Step back and finish with toma katate uchi and zanshin (pic. 8-12).

Aiki-jo kihons · kaeshi tsuki - kihon #3

Begin in left profile stance. Execute kaeshi tsuki off the line (pic. 1-4). Continue with ue no uke nagashi with a pull back. Take over the front end of the jo and finish with kaeshi and zanshin (pic. 5-10).

Aiki-jo kihons · kaeshi tsuki - kihon #4

Begin in left profile stance. Execute kaeshi tsuki off the line (pic. 1-4). Continue with ue no uke nagashi with a pull back (pic. 5-6). Step forward and follow with toma katate uchi. Transition into ue no uke nagashi and finish with kaeshi and zanshin (pic. 7-13).

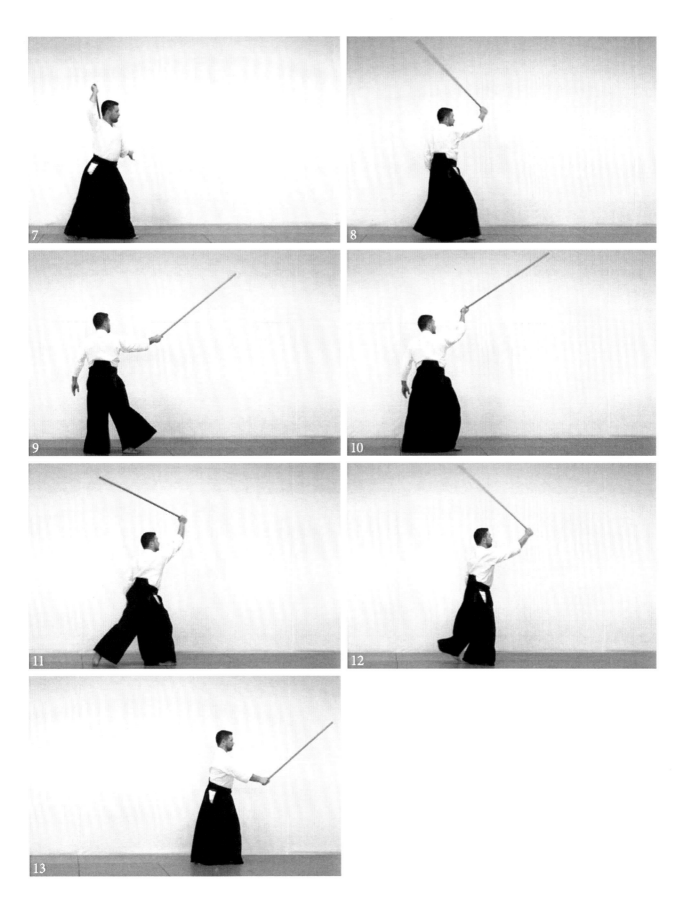

Aiki-jo kihons · kaeshi tsuki - kihon #5

Begin in left profile stance. Execute kaeshi tsuki off the line (pic. 1-4). Continue with ue no uke nagashi with a pull back (pic. 5-6). Follow with toma katate uchi with pass over, and return with kaeshi and zanshin at the end (pic. 8-13).

Aiki-jo kihons · kaeshi tsuki - kihon #6

Begin in left profile stance. Execute kaeshi tsuki off the line (pic. 1-3). Continue with ue no uke nagashi with a pull back (pic. 4-5). Follow with toma katate uchi, transition into shita no uke nagashi, and finish with tsuki jodan and zanshin (pic. 9-12).

Aiki-jo kihons · kaeshi tsuki - kihon #7

Begin in left profile stance. Execute kaeshi tsuki off the line (pic. 1-3). Continue with ue no uke nagashi with a pull back (pic. 4-5). Follow with toma katate uchi and twist your upper body in place. Pull the jo back and take over the front end of the jo (pic. 6-10). Finish with kaeshi and zanshin (pic. 11-12).

Explore Aikido Vol. 2

Aiki-jo kihons · kaeshi tsuki - kihon #8

Begin in left profile stance. Execute kaeshi tsuki off the line (pic. 1-3). Continue with ue no uke nagashi with a pull back (pic. 4-5). Follow with toma katate uchi and bring the front end of the jo to the back (pic. 6-9). With a slight delay, execute tsuki jodan and zanshin (pic. 10-12).

Explore Aikido Vol. 2

Aiki-jo kihons · kaeshi tsuki - kihon #9

Begin in left profile stance. Execute kaeshi tsuki off the line (pic. 1-3). Continue with ue no uke nagashi with a pull back (pic. 4-5). Follow with toma katate uchi with pass over and use your left hand to take hold of the end of the jo (pic. 6-9). Step forward and execute tsuki jodan with zanshin (pic. 10-12).

Aiki-jo kihons · kaeshi tsuki - kihon #10

Begin in left profile stance. Execute kaeshi tsuki off the line (pic. 1-3). Continue with shita no uke nagashi (pic. 4-5). Finish with tsuki jodan and zanshin (pic. 6-8).

Aiki-jo kihons · kaeshi tsuki - kihon #11

Begin in left profile stance. Execute kaeshi tsuki off the line (pic. 1-4). Immediately retract the jo and return with a vertical kaeshi tsuki (pic. 5-8).

Aiki-jo kihons · kaeshi tsuki - kihon #12

Begin in left profile stance. Execute kaeshi tsuki off the line (pic. 1-3). Continue with ue no uke nagashi (pic. 4-5). Follow with toma katate uchi. Pass over, step forward, and return with kaeshi and zanshin (6-11).

Aiki-jo kihons · kaeshi tsuki - kihon #13

Begin in left profile stance. With your right hand, thumb down, take over the top end of the jo (pic. 1-2). Execute toma katate uchi, initially onto jodan level and then gedan (pic. 3-6). Finish with kaeshi and zanshin (pic. 10-13).

Aiki-jo kihons · kaeshi tsuki - kihon #14

Begin in left profile stance. With your right hand, thumb down, take over the top end of the jo (pic. 1-2). Execute toma katate uchi (pic. 3-5). Continue with ue no uke nagashi and finish with kaeshi and zanshin (pic. 6-9).

Aiki-jo kihons · kaeshi tsuki - kihon #15

Begin in left profile stance. With your right hand, thumb down, take over the top end of the jo (pic. 1-2). Execute toma katate uchi (pic. 3-5). Continue with shita no uke nagashi and finish with tsuki jodan and zanshin (pic. 6-9).

Furi Komi Kihons

Aiki-jo kihons · furi komi - base kihon

This furi komi tsuki kihon is a base, or a primary kihon, without a number. There are fifteen furi komi tsuki kihons that follow.

Begin in left profile stance. Execute furi komi tsuki off the line (pic. 1-4). Strike down at the wrist level (pic. 5-6). Move forward and finish with tsuki and zanshin (pic. 7-8).

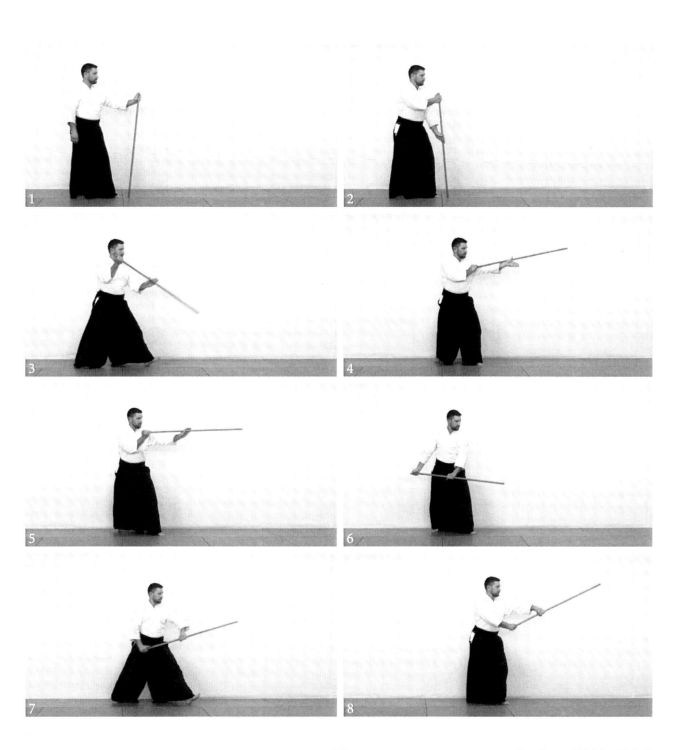

Aiki-jo kihons · furi komi - kihon #1

Begin in left profile stance. Execute furi komi tsuki off the line (pic. 1-4). Strike down at the wrist level and continue hasso gaeshi (pic. 5-8). From hasso no kamae, enter forward with men uchi and zanshin at the end (pic. 9-12).

Aiki-jo kihons · furi komi - kihon #2

Begin in left profile stance. Execute furi komi tsuki off the line (pic. 1-3). Strike down at the wrist level and continue hasso gaeshi (pic. 5-7). From hasso no kamae, continue with men uchi (pic. 8-9). Follow with ue no uke nagashi and finish with kaeshi and zanshin (pic. 10-12).

Explore Aikido Vol. 2

Aiki-jo kihons · furi komi - kihon #3

Begin in left profile stance. Execute furi komi tsuki off the line (pic. 1-4). Strike down at the wrist level and continue hasso gaeshi (pic. 5-7). From hasso no kamae step forward with men uchi (pic. 8-9). Follow with shita no uke nagashi and finish with tsuki jodan and zanshin (pic. 10-12).

Aiki-jo kihons · furi komi - kihon #4

Begin in left profile stance. Execute furi komi tsuki off the line (pic. 1-4). Strike down at the wrist level and continue hasso gaeshi (pic. 5-7). From hasso no kamae step forward with furi komi tsuki (pic. 8-9). Follow with furi komi no uke nagashi and finish with kaeshi and zanshin (pic. 10-12).

Explore Aikido Vol. 2

Aiki-jo kihons · furi komi - kihon #5

Begin in left profile stance. Execute furi komi tsuki off the line (pic. 1-3). Strike down at the wrist level and continue hasso gaeshi (pic. 4-6). From hasso no kamae step forward with men uchi (pic. 7-8). Retract the jo and execute furi komi tsuki (pic. 9-11). Strike down at the wrist level and finish with tsuki jodan and zanshin (pic. 7-8).

Aiki-jo kihons · furi komi - kihon #6

Begin in left profile stance. Execute furi komi tsuki off the line (pic. 1-3). Strike down at the wrist level and continue hasso gaeshi (pic. 4-6). From hasso no kamae step forward with men uchi (pic. 7-8). Retract the jo and execute choku tsuki and zanshin (pic. 9-11).

Aiki-jo kihons · furi komi - kihon #7

Begin in left profile stance. Execute furi komi tsuki off the line (pic. 1-4). Execute short form of ue no uke nagashi and return with kaeshi and zanshin (pic. 5-8).

Aiki-jo kihons · furi komi - kihon #8

Begin in left profile stance. Execute furi komi tsuki off the line (pic. 1-3). Strike down at the wrist level and continue hasso gaeshi (pic. 4-6). From hasso no kamae step forward with furi komi tsuki (pic. 7-9). Pull and redirect the jo to gedan level and finish with tsuki jodan and zanshin (pic. 10-14).

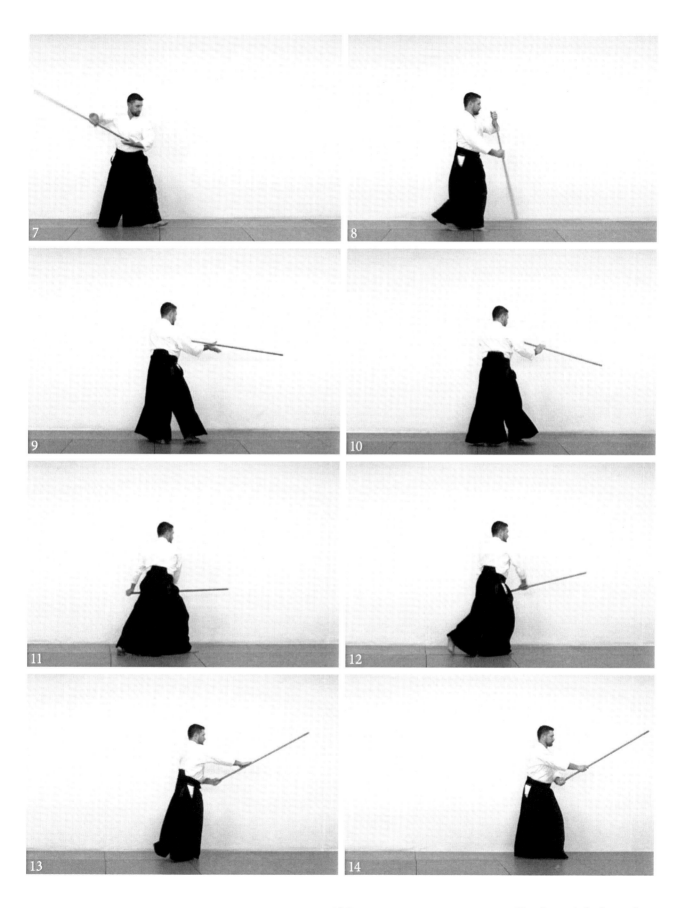

Aiki-jo kihons · furi komi - kihon #9

Begin in left profile stance. Execute furi komi tsuki off the line (pic. 1-3). Strike down at the wrist level and continue hasso gaeshi (pic. 4-6). From hasso no kamae step forward with men uchi (pic. 7-8). Retract the jo and finish with kaeshi tsuki and zanshin (pic. 9-12).

Explore Aikido Vol. 2

Aiki-jo kihons · furi komi - kihon #10

Begin in left profile stance. Execute furi komi tsuki off the line (pic. 1-3). Strike down at the wrist level and continue hasso gaeshi (pic. 4-5). From hasso no kamae step forward with men uchi (pic. 6-7). Retract the jo and execute furi komi tsuki (pic. 8-10). Pull and redirect the jo to gedan level and finish with tsuki jodan and zanshin (pic. 11-14).

Aiki-jo kihons · furi komi - kihon #11

Begin in left profile stance. Execute furi komi tsuki off the line (pic. 1-3). Strike down at the wrist level and continue hasso gaeshi (pic. 4-6). From hasso no kamae step forward with men uchi (pic. 7-8). Retract the jo and execute choku tsuki (pic. 9-11). Follow with another tsuki no uke nagashi and finish with tsuki jodan and zanshin (pic. 12-14).

Aiki-jo kihons · furi komi - kihon #12

Begin in left profile stance. Execute furi komi tsuki off the line (pic. 1-3). Execute short version of ue no uke nagashi and return with kaeshi (pic. 5-8). Continue with quick uke nagashi and kaeshi with zanshin at the end (pic. 9-12).

Aiki-jo kihons · furi komi - kihon #13

Begin in left profile stance. Execute furi komi tsuki off the line (pic. 1-3). Continue with ue no uke nagashi with a pull back (pic. 4-5). Follow with toma katate uchi, initially onto jodan level, then gedan. Transition to ue no uke nagashi and finish with kaeshi and zanshin (pic. 10-13).

Aiki-jo kihons · furi komi - kihon #14

Begin in left profile stance. Execute furi komi tsuki off the line (pic. 1-3). Continue with ue no uke nagashi with a pull back (pic. 4-5). Follow with toma katate uchi, transition to ue no uke nagashi, and finish with kaeshi and zanshin (pic. 6-13).

Aiki-jo kihons · furi komi - kihon #15

Begin in left profile stance. Execute furi komi tsuki off the line (pic. 1-4). Continue with ue no uke nagashi with a pull back (pic. 5-6). Follow with toma katate uchi, transition to shita no uke nagashi, and finish with tsuki jodan and zanshin (pic. 7-13).

Two Direction Kihons

Aiki-jo kihons · two direction kihon #1

The following choku tsuki kihon is applicable against two opponents. It consist of elements that were included and explained on previous pages. There won't be any written explanation for this kihon. As you become familiar with the basic aiki-jo suburi and kihons showcased earlier, it will be easier to reproduce this kihon. Please view the two direction long kihon on the following pages (pic. 1-50).

Aiki-jo kihons · two direction kihon #2

The following first kaeshi tsuki kihon is applicable against two opponents. It consists of elements that were included and explained on previous pages. Here is the second two direction kihon (pic. 1-19).

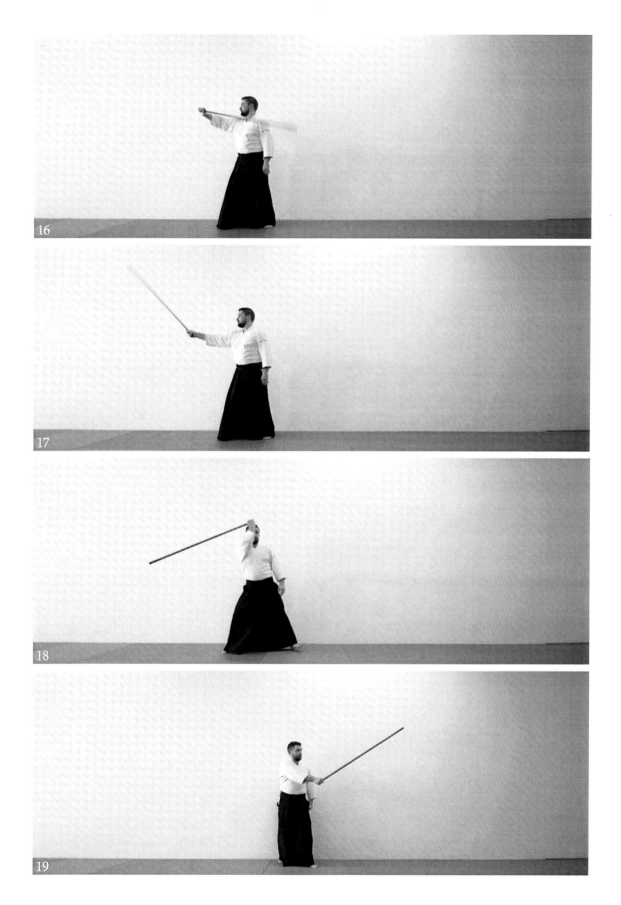

Aiki-jo kihons · two direction kihon #3.

The following second kaeshi tsuki kihon is applicable against two opponents. It consist of elements that were included and explained on previous pages. Here is the third two direction kihon (pic. 1-27).

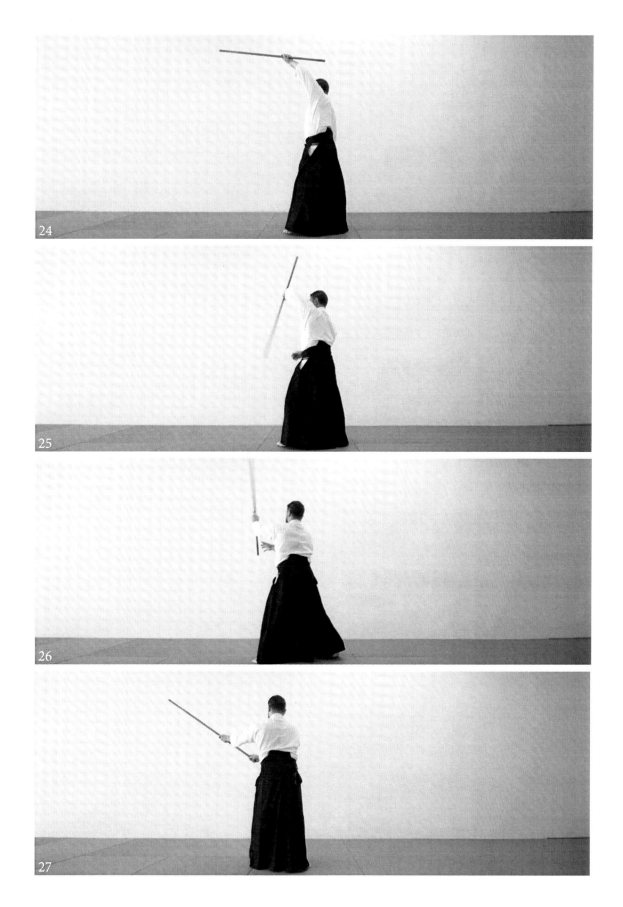

Aiki-jo kihons · two direction kihon #4.

The following furi komi tsuki kihon is applicable against two opponents. It consists of elements that were included and explained on previous pages. Here is the fourth two direction kihon (pic. 1-19).

Jo Nage

Throughout jo nage techniques there should be a permanent center line control until uke connects. This causes uke to follow and try to catch the jo. Also, you shouldn't allow uke to catch the jo too early, as it would be more challenging to execute the technique.

Jo nage - kokyu nage

Begin by offering your jo to uke slightly off the line (pic. 1-2). As uke approaches and is about to catch the jo, absorb uke by moving slightly back, simultaneously pull the jo up in a similar way to ue no uke nagashi (pic. 3-4). As uke connects, push the jo forward and execute kokyu nage (pic. 5-8).

Jo nage - shiho nage sankyo

Begin by offering your jo to uke slightly off the line (pic. 1). As uke approaches and is about to catch the jo, absorb uke in by moving back, and smoothly drop the front end of the jo down (pic. 2-3). As uke connects, pull uke slightly forward and create a large circle projected above and behind uke, and finish shiho nage sankyo (pic. 4-8).

Explore Aikido Vol. 2

Jo nage - irimi nage

Begin by offering your jo to uke slightly off the line (pic. 1). As uke approaches and is about to catch the jo, absorb uke by moving slightly back and off the line. At the same time, retract the jo halfway into your left hand (pic. 2-3). Step forward and execute direct irimi nage (pic. 4-8).

Jo nage - "paddle" irimi nage

Begin by offering your jo to uke slightly off the line (pic. 1). As uke approaches and is about to catch the jo, absorb uke by stepping back and off the line. At the same time, retract the jo, release its back end, and place it flat onto uke's neck (pic. 2-3). Use the jo to pull uke down, and with a circular jo maneuver, similar to paddling, bring uke around (pic. 4-6). Once uke is up, step forward with the jo attached flat to uke's neck, and finish irimi nage (pic. 7-8).

Jo nage - yoko irimi

Begin by offering your jo to uke slightly off the line (pic. 1). As uke approaches and is about to catch the jo, absorb uke by retracting the jo all the way back and change profile (pic. 2-3). As uke is in reachable distance, release approximately 1/3 of the jo's length. Step forward and place the extended jo and your forearm onto uke's neck, so that it creates a "V" shaped enclosure (pic. 4). Squeeze the jo and your forearm together, push back, then release uke's neck (pic. 5-7). Zanshin at the end is optional within all jo nage techniques (pic. 8).

Jo nage - irimi nage - variation with a neck lock

Begin by offering your jo to uke slightly off the line (pic. 1). As uke approaches and is about to catch the jo, absorb uke by moving slightly back. Pull the jo, changing the front hand grip and placing it in the middle of the jo. Move forward and place the extended front part of the jo and your forearm behind uke's neck, so it creates a "V" shaped enclosure (pic. 2-5). Squeeze the jo and your forearm

together and pull uke with you into a circular motion (pic. 6-7). Release the hold and execute irimi nage with your forearm (pic. 8-10). You may exercise zanshin at the end (pic. 11-12).

Jo nage - nikyo

Begin by offering your jo to uke slightly off the line. As uke approaches and is about to catch the jo, absorb uke by moving slightly back. As uke connects, wrap the jo around his back hand wrist (pic. 1-3). Push the jo directly toward uke's center and execute nikyo (pic. 4-6). Zanshin at the end is optional (pic. 7-8).

Explore Aikido Vol. 2

Jo nage - shiho nage

Begin by offering your jo to uke slightly off the line. As uke approaches and is about to catch the jo, push the jo sideways and redirect uke to create an opening for shiho nage (pic. 1-2). Simultaneously pull uke forward, enter under the jo, and execute shiho nage (pic. 3-8).

Jo nage - kaiten nage

Begin by offering your jo to uke slightly off the line (pic. 1). As uke approaches and is about to catch the jo, pull uke up and at the same time reposition your grip at 1/3 of the jo's length (pic. 2-4). Hook the bottom part of the jo on uke's inner thigh. Execute kaiten nage by rotating the jo in a circular, "steering wheel" like motion (pic. 5-8).

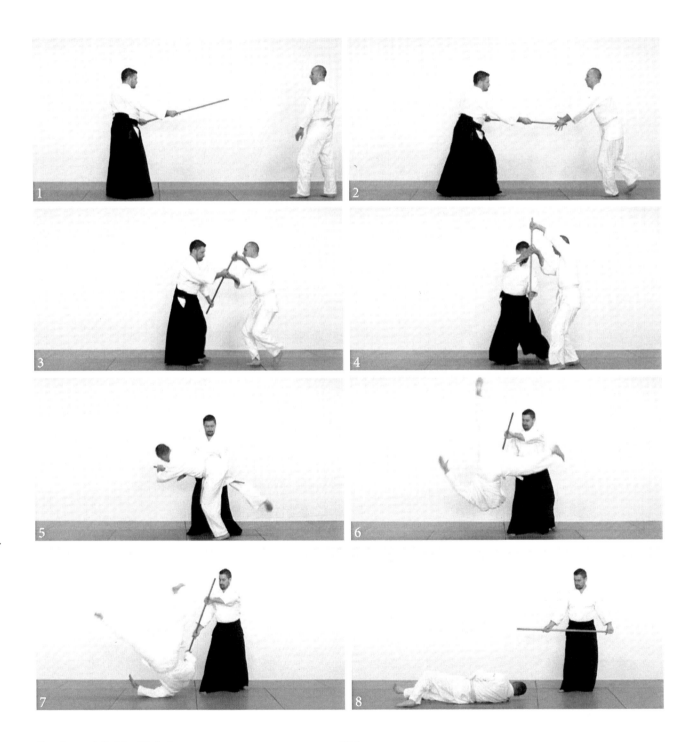

Explore Aikido Vol. 2

Jo nage - sudori nage

Begin by offering your jo to uke slightly off the line (pic. 1). As uke approaches and is about to catch the jo, pull uke up by bringing the jo high (pic. 2). Once uke is in kuzushi, continue with the jo in a circular motion into uke's shin(s) and finish sudori nage (pic. 3-8).

Jo nage - "loop" kokyu nage

Begin by offering your jo to uke slightly off the line. As uke approaches and is about to catch the jo, absorb uke by moving back. Bring the jo in with you and down. Before uke catches the jo, make a loop, so that uke follows and changes direction (pic. 1-3). Pull uke forward. Once uke passes by and under the jo (pic. 4), pull the jo down and execute the technique (pic. 5-6). Zanshin at the end is optional (pic. 7-8).

Jo nage - koshi nage

Begin by offering your jo to uke slightly off the line (pic. 1). As uke approaches and is about to catch the jo, push the jo sideways and redirect uke to create an opening for the entry (pic. 2-3). Move forward and under and load uke onto your hips (pic. 4-5). Rise and execute koshi nage (pic. 6-8).

Jo nage - aiki otoshi

Begin by offering your jo to uke slightly off the line (pic. 1). As uke approaches and is about to catch the jo, absorb uke by moving back. Pull the jo up in a similar way to ue no uke nagashi (pic. 2-3). As uke comes into reachable distance, escape with the jo in a circular motion and return strike, aiming at uke's Achilles tendon(s), and finish aiki otoshi (pic. 4-8).

Jo nage - kokyu nage - variation with offering back end of the jo

Begin by offering your jo to uke slightly off the line (pic. 1). As uke approaches and is about to catch the jo, absorb uke by changing your profile position and simultaneously retracting and pulling the jo away from uke (pic. 2-3). As uke comes into reachable distance, release the back end of the jo and "offer" it on uke's center line for uke to grab (pic. 4). Pull uke forward and finish kokyu nage (pic. 5-8).

The following techniques are ushiro in a sense that we turn away and uke approaches from behind.

Jo nage - ushiro irimi nage

Begin by offering your jo to uke slightly off the line (pic. 1). As uke approaches and is about to catch the jo, absorb uke by retracting your jo all the way in and simultaneously turning away and off the line (pic. 2-3). As uke comes into reachable distance, turn around and release the back end of the jo onto uke's center line and finish irimi nage (pic. 4-6). Zanshin at the end is optional (pic. 7-8).

Explore Aikido Vol. 2

Jo nage - ushiro yoko irimi

Begin by offering your jo to uke slightly off the line (pic. 1). As uke approaches and is about to catch the jo, absorb uke by retracting your jo all the way in. Simultaneously turn away and off the line, and release the back end of the jo in front of uke (pic. 2-3). Let uke catch the jo, then pull it forward. Once uke passes by and under the jo, execute yoko irimi (pic. 4-7). Zanshin at the end is optional (pic. 8).

Jo nage - ushiro kokyu nage #1

Begin by offering your jo to uke slightly off the line (pic. 1). As uke approaches and is about to catch the jo, absorb uke by retracting your jo all the way in. Simultaneously turn away and off the line, then release the back end of the jo in front of uke (pic. 2-4). Once uke connects, bring uke forward and finish kokyu nage (pic. 5-8). Zanshin at the end is optional (pic. 9-10).

Explore Aikido Vol. 2

Jo nage - ushiro kokyu nage #2

Begin by offering your jo to uke slightly off the line (pic. 1). As uke approaches and is about to catch the jo, absorb uke by retracting the jo all the way in. Simultaneously turn away and off the line, then release the back end of the jo perpendicular to uke's direction (pic. 2-3). Once uke connects, change the direction by creating loop-like trajectory, bring uke forward, and finish kokyu nage (pic. 4-9). Zanshin at the end is optional (pic. 10).

Jo nage - ushiro sudori nage

Begin by offering your jo to uke slightly off the line (pic. 1). As uke approaches and is about to catch the jo, absorb uke by retracting the jo all the way in. Simultaneously turn away and off the line, then offer the back end of the jo up high, perpendicular to uke's direction (pic. 2-4). Once uke is in kuzushi, return with the jo in a circular trajectory into uke's shin(s) and execute sudori nage (pic. 5-9). Zanshin at the end is optional (pic. 10).

Explore Aikido Vol. 2

Jo nage - ushiro shiho nage sankyo

Begin by offering your jo to uke slightly off the line (pic. 1). As uke approaches and is about to catch the jo, absorb uke by retracting the jo all the way in. Simultaneously turn away and off the line, then release the back end of the jo perpendicular to uke's direction (pic. 2-4). As uke connects, change direction by creating loop-like trajectory (pic. 5-6). Once uke comes around from the loop and passes by and under the jo, execute shiho nage sankyo (pic. 7-9). Zanshin at the end is optional (pic. 10).

Explore Aikido Vol. 2

Jo nage - ushiro "compact" irimi nage

Begin by offering your jo to uke slightly off the line (pic. 1). As uke approaches and is about to catch the jo, absorb uke by retracting the jo all the way in. Simultaneously turn away and off the line, then release the back end of the jo perpendicular to uke's direction (pic. 2-3). As uke connects, change direction by looping the trajectory (pic. 4-5). Once uke comes around from the loop, immediately step forward with the jo perpendicular to uke's direction, and finish irimi nage (pic. 6-9). Zanshin at the end is optional (pic. 10).

Jo Dori

Jo dori - irimi nage

Uke, in right profile stance, starts with choku tsuki judan. From left profile position, simultaneously move forward and off the line, and use your left hand to deflect the jo (pic. 1-3). Step in and execute irimi nage (pic. 4-8).

Jo dori - ikkyo omote

Uke, in left profile stance, starts with choku tsuki judan. From right profile position step back, at the same time, use your right hand to deflect the jo (pic. 1-4). With your left hand, take control of both uke's left hand grip and the jo, and execute ikkyo omote (pic. 5-9). Zanshin at the end is optional (pic. 10).

Jo dori - nikyo ura

Uke, in left profile stance, starts with choku tsuki judan. From right profile position step back and use both hands to take hold of the jo (pic. 1-4). Wrap the back end of the jo around uke's right wrist and execute nikyo ura toward uke's center (pic. 5-9). Zanshin at the end is optional (pic. 9-10).

Jo dori - sankyo omote

Uke, in left profile stance, starts with choku tsuki judan. From right profile position step back. At the same time, use your right hand to deflect the jo and your left hand to take control of both uke's front hand grip and the jo (pic. 1-4). Position uke in transitional ikkyo (pic. 5-6). With your right hand take over uke's left wrist and finish sankyo omote (pic. 7-10). Zanshin at the end is optional (pic. 10-11).

Jo dori - kotegaeshi

Uke, in right profile stance, starts with choku tsuki judan. From left profile position, move forward and off the line. Use your left hand to deflect the jo and take over both uke's right hand grip and the jo. With your right hand apply atemi (pic. 1-4). Pull uke forward into kuzushi and execute kotegaeshi (pic. 5-10). Zanshin at the end is optional (pic. 11-12).

Explore Aikido Vol. 2

Jo dori - ude kime nage

Uke, in right profile stance, starts with choku tsuki judan. From right profile position, simultaneously move back. With your right hand, take over both uke's right hand grip and the jo. Pull uke forward and execute ude kime nage (pic. 1-8). Zanshin at the end is optional (pic. 9-10).

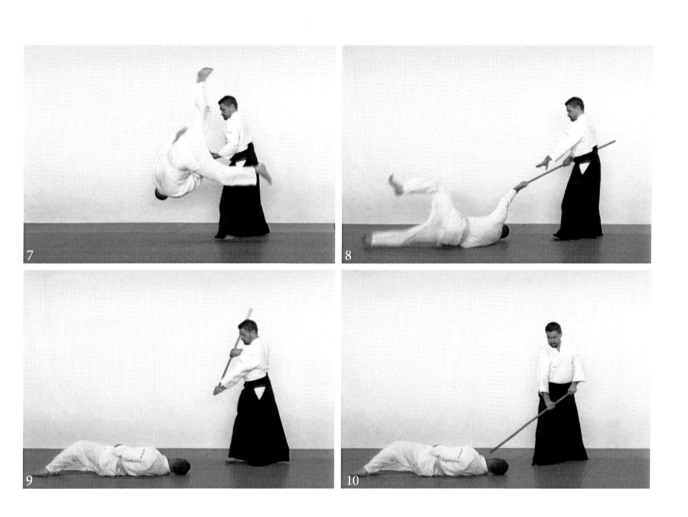

Jo dori - sumi otoshi

Uke, in left profile stance, starts with choku tsuki judan. From right profile stance, simultaneously step back and use both hands to take control of the jo (pic. 1-4). Wrap the jo from inside out over uke's left elbow pit and execute sumi otoshi (pic. 5-8). Zanshin at the end is optional (pic. 9-10).

Jo dori - yoko irimi

Uke, in right profile stance, starts with choku tsuki judan. From left profile stance, simultaneously move back. With your left hand, deflect the jo, regrab it with your right hand close to uke's front hand grip, and bring uke forward (pic. 1-6). Once uke passes by, execute yoko irimi (pic. 7-10). Zanshin at the end is optional (pic. 11).

Jo dori - juji garami

Uke, in right profile stance, starts with choku tsuki judan. From right profile stance, simultaneously shift back and off the line, and use your right hand to deflect and take hold of the jo (pic. 1-4). With a circular movement, bring the jo to the front, add your left hand hold to the jo, wrap uke's arms one over the other, and execute juji garami (pic. 5-9). Zanshin at the end is optional (pic. 10-11).

Jo dori - shiho nage sankyo

Uke, in right profile stance, starts with choku tsuki judan. From left profile position, simultaneously move back and off the line. Use your left hand to deflect and take hold of the jo. Add your right hand hold to the jo (pic. 1-4). With a circular movement and step forward, bring the jo above and behind uke and execute shiho nage sankyo (pic. 5-8). Zanshin at the end is optional (pic. 9-10).

Jo dori - gokyo

Uke, in left profile stance, starts with choku tsuki judan. From right profile position, simultaneously step back, and use your left hand to deflect and take hold of the jo (pic. 1-4). Step back again, transfer the jo to the other side, use your right hand to take control of uke's left elbow, and finish gokyo (pic. 5-10).

Jo dori - kokyu nage

Uke, in right profile stance, starts with choku tsuki judan. From right profile stance, simultaneously step back and off the line, and use both hands to take hold of the jo (pic. 1-4). With movement similar to ue no uke nagashi, bring uke forward and execute kokyu nage (pic. 5-8). Zanshin at the end is optional (pic. 9-10).

Kumi Jo

Kumi jo · choku tsuki - base kihon

Both shite and seme begin in left profile stance (pic. 1). Seme attacks with choku tsuki judan, and shite counters with choku tsuki judan off the line (pic. 1-3). Shite continues and attacks seme's back hand grip (pic. 4-6). Shite exercises tsuki jodan and zanshin (pic. 7). The kihon ends when seme lowers the jo down (pic. 8).

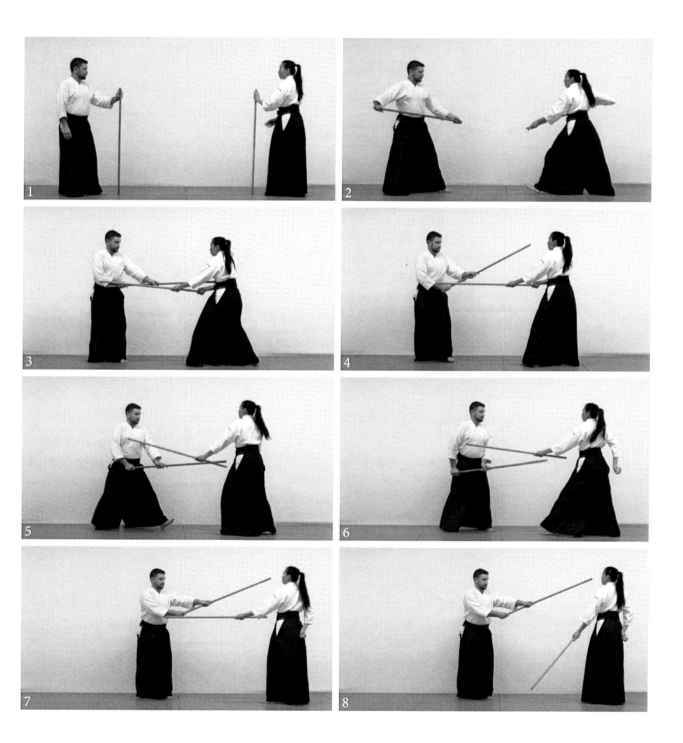

Kumi jo · choku tsuki - kihon #1

Both shite and seme begin in left profile stance (pic. 1). Seme attacks with choku tsuki judan, and shite counters with choku tsuki judan off the line (pic. 2-5). Seme moves back and tries to block shite's counter attack. At the same time, shite executes ue no uke nagashi and exposes his position (pic. 6-8). As seme releases choku tsuki judan, shite counters with choku tsuki jodan in full extension, which seme avoids with ue no uke nagashi and by moving back (pic. 9-10). Shite continues with men strike which seme attempts to block (pic. 11-13). Shite transitions to ue no uke nagashi and finishes with kaeshi and zanshin (pic. 14-15). Kihon ends when seme lowers the jo down (pic. 16).

Explore Aikido Vol. 2

Kumi jo · choku tsuki - kihon #6

Shite begins in left profile stance with the jo in right hand; seme begins in right profile stance with the jo in both hands ready to attack (pic. 1). Seme attacks with shomen uchi and shite moves forward and counters with choku tsuki jodan (pic. 2-6). Seme moves back to avoid the thrust, and shite continues with ue no uke nagashi. Seme regains stability and counters with shomen uchi. Shite applies final kaeshi strike and zanshin (pic. 7-10). Kihon ends when seme lowers the jo down (pic. 11).

Kumi jo · choku tsuki - kihon #12

Both shite and seme begin in left profile stance (pic. 1). Seme attacks with choku tsuki judan, and shite counters with choku tsuki judan off the line (pic. 1-5). Seme moves back and tries to block shite's counter attack. At the same time, shite retracts the jo all the way in and continues with a gedan kaeshi strike to the knee, which seme tries to block (pic. 6-8). Shite redirects the jo into judan level and enters with tsuki jodan and zanshin at the end (pic. 9-11). Kihon ends when seme lowers the jo down (pic. 12).

Explore Aikido Vol. 2

Kumi jo · kaeshi tsuki - base kihon

Both shite and seme begin in left profile stance (pic. 1). Seme attacks with choku tsuki judan. Shite counters with kaeshi tsuki off the line (pic. 2-5). Shite continues and attacks seme's front hand (pic. 6). Shite executes tsuki jodan and zanshin (pic. 7-8). Kihon ends when seme lowers the jo down (pic. 9).

Explore Aikido Vol. 2

Kumi jo · kaeshi tsuki - kihon #1

Both shite and seme begin in left profile stance (pic. 1). Seme attacks with choku tsuki judan, and shite counters with kaeshi tsuki off the line (pic. 2-4). To avoid the strike, seme moves back and tries to block the strike. Shite executes ue no uke nagashi with a pull back and immediately steps forward with toma katate uchi and zanshin (pic. 5-9). Kihon ends when seme lowers the jo down (pic. 10).

Explore Aikido Vol. 2

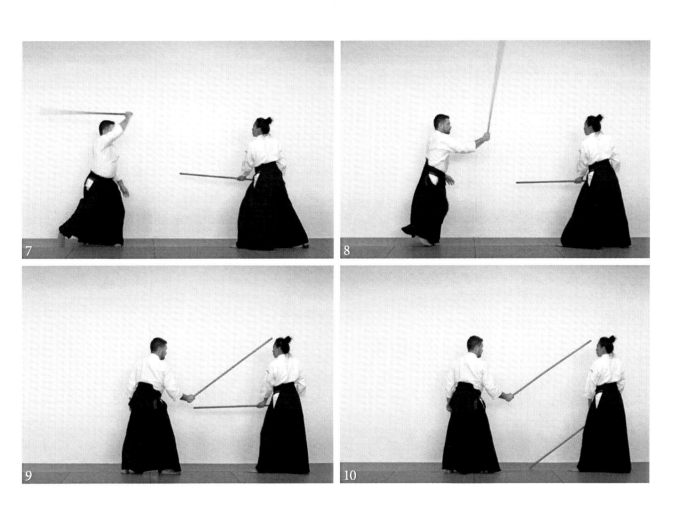

Kumi jo · kaeshi tsuki - kihon #3

Both shite and seme begin in left profile stance (pic. 1). Seme attacks with choku tsuki judan. Shite counters with kaeshi tsuki off the line (pic. 1-4). To avoid the strike, seme moves back and tries to block the strike. Shite avoids the block by moving back and executing ue no uke nagashi (pic. 5-7). Seme continues and attacks with choku tsuki judan, and shite finishes with kaeshi and zanshin (pic. 8-9). Kihon ends when seme lowers the jo down (pic. 10).

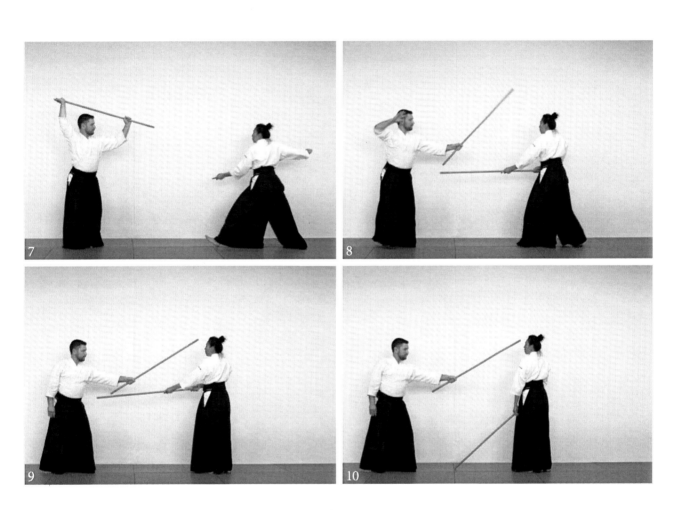

Kumi jo · kaeshi tsuki - kihon #8

Both shite and seme begin in left profile stance (pic. 1). Seme attacks with choku tsuki judan, and shite counters with kaeshi tsuki off the line (pic. 1-3). To avoid the strike, seme moves back and tries to block the strike. Shite executes ue no uke nagashi and follows with toma katate uchi (pic. 4-7). Seme shifts back and tries to block the strike. Shite passes over with toma katate uchi and brings the jo back (pic. 8-9). Seme attacks with tsuki judan, shite moves forward and counters with tsuki jodan and zanshin (pic. 10-13). Kihon ends when seme lowers the jo down (pic. 14).

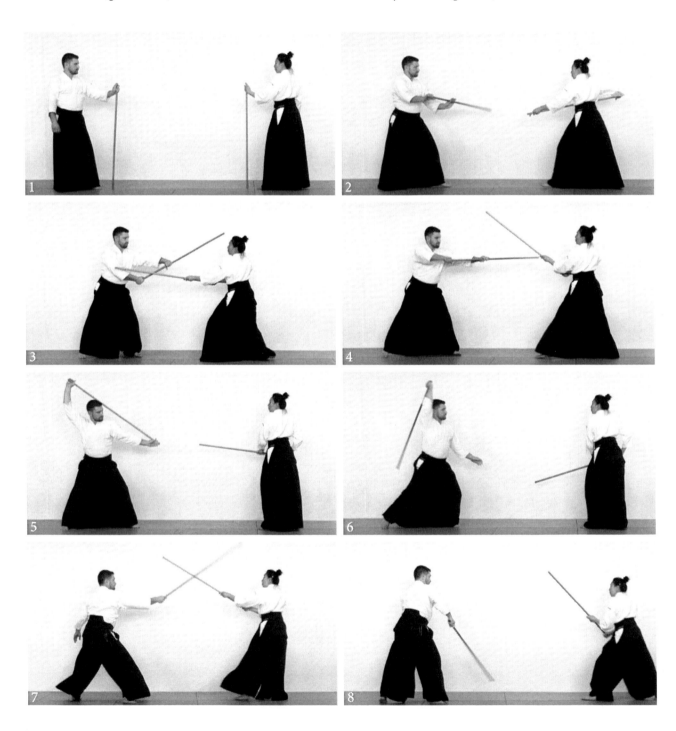

Kumi jo · furi komi tsuki - base kihon

Both shite and seme begin in left profile stance (pic. 1). Seme attacks with choku tsuki judan, and shite counters with furi komi tsuki off the line (pic. 1-4). Shite continues and attacks seme's front hand (pic. 5-7). Shite finishes with tsuki jodan and zanshin (pic. 8-9). Kihon ends when seme lowers the jo down (pic. 10).

Kumi jo · furi komi tsuki - kihon #1

Both shite and seme begin in left profile stance (pic. 1). Seme attacks with choku tsuki judan, and shite counters with furi komi tsuki off the line (pic. 1-3). Shite attacks seme's front hand and executes hasso kaeshi (pic. 4-7). Shite immediately steps forward, strikes shomen uchi and finishes with zanshin (pic. 8-10). Kihon ends when seme lowers the jo down (pic. 11).

Explore Aikido Vol. 2

Kumi jo · furi komi tsuki - kihon #4

Both shite and seme begin in left profile stance (pic. 1). Seme attacks with choku tsuki judan. Shite counters with furi komi tsuki off the line (pic. 1-3). Shite attacks seme's front hand and executes hasso kaeshi (pic. 4-6). Shite immediately steps forward with furi komi tsuki, which seme attempts to block (pic. 7-8). Shite responds with furi komi no uke nagashi and kaeshi with zanshin (pic. 9-11). Kihon ends when seme lowers the jo down (pic. 11).

Kumi jo · furi komi tsuki - kihon #13

Both shite and seme begin in left profile stance (pic. 1). Seme attacks with choku tsuki judan, and shite counters with furi komi tsuki off the line (pic. 2-3). To avoid the thrust, seme moves back and tries to block it. Shite executes ue no uke nagashi and immediate toma katate uchi, initially jodan and then gedan. Seme attempts to avoid and block both strikes (pic. 4-8). Shite responds with ue no uke nagashi and kaeshi with zanshin (pic. 9-11). Kihon ends when seme lowers the jo down (pic. 12).

Explore Aikido Vol. 2

Japanese - English Glossary

Ai - harmony
aiki-jo - aikido training with wooden staff
aiki-ken - aikido training with wooden sword
arigato - thanks, thank you
ashi - foot, leg
ashikubi - ankle
atemi - strike, blow
ayumi ashi - regular step, ordinary walking, where the legs move forward alternately

Bokken - wooden sword
budo - Japanese martial arts
bushi - warrior
bushido - feudal-military Japanese code of behavior followed by the samurai

Chikama - shortest distance, face to face with the opponent
chudan - middle position

Dan - black belt rank
deshi - student
do - way, path
dojo - martial arts studio
dojo cho - chief instructor
domo arigato gozaimashita - thank you very much (used after each class to your partner and sensei)
dori - grab, hold

Futari Dori - training against two opponents

Geri - kick
gedan - lower position
godan - 5th degree black belt rank
gyakuhanmi - opposite stance, mirrored stance

Ha - edge of bokken's blade
hachidan - 8th degree black belt rank
hai - yes
hakama - traditional Japanese pants usually worn by black belt ranks or senior students
hara - abdomen
hanmi handachi waza - aikido practice in a seated position against standing attacker(s)
hidari - left
hiji - elbow
hiza - knee

Irimi - entering movement
irimi nage - entering throw, one of the fundamental aikido techniques

Jo - wooden staff
jo dori - techniques against uke equipped/attacking with jo.
jo omote - take your jo
jo ite - place your jo away
jodan - upper position
judan - 10th degree black belt rank

Kaeshi waza - counter techniques
kai - organization
kamae - position, stance
kamiza - an alter, place of honor. In the dojo it refers to a place where the portrait(s) of the school predecessor(s) and/or calligraphy scroll is displayed
kashira - back end of bokken's handle
keiko - training
ken dori - techniques for disarming an opponent equipped with bokken
ki - mind, spirit, energy
kihon - basic form
kensaki - tip of the bokken's blade
kokoro - heart, spirit
kokyuho - way or method of breathing
kokyu nage - "breath throw" techniques
kote - wrist
kotegaeshi - outward wrist turn or twist
kubi - neck
kuzushi - off balance position/unbalancing the opponent
kyu - any rank below black belt
kyudan - 9th degree black belt rank

Ma-ai - correct, proper distance
mae - front
meguri - flexibility and rotation of the forearms
men - face
mokuso - meditation
mono uchi - 6-8 inches of the blade closest to the sword's / bokken's tip
mune - 1) chest; 2) back of the bokken's blade
mushin - lit. no mind

Nage - throw
nanadan - 7th degree black belt rank
nanakyo - seventh pin
nidan - 2nd degree black belt rank
Nippon - Japan

O - grand, big
O'Sensei - grand master, in aikido this title refers to the founder of aikido, Morihei Ueshiba
obi - belt
omote - in the front direction (in aikido we can divide techniques into omote and ura)
onegai shimasu - in aikido training it is used at the beginning of each class and it can be understood as "please let me train with you"

Rei - bow
rokudan - 6th degree black belt rank
ryu - in budo it refers to school or style

Sandan - 3rd degree black belt rank
saya - scabbard
shiho nage - throw in four directions
seika tanden - central point of stomach located slightly below the navel
shikko - knee walking
seiza - kneeling seated position
seme - attacker, term especially used during aiki-ken and aiki-jo training. In aiki-tai jutsu the term would be replaced with "uke"
sensei - teacher, master, instructor
shite - defender, term especially used during aiki-ken and aiki-jo training. In aiki-tai jutsu the term is replaced with "tori"
shihan - master instructor
shinogi - bokken's blade ridge
shodan - 1st degree black belt rank
shomen - front or top of head
sode - sleeve
soto - outside, on the outside
suburi - basic jo or bokken practice in striking and thrusting
suwari waza - techniques in sitting position

Tachi waza - standing techniques
tai sabaki - body movements related to specific aikido techniques
tai jutsu - the art of the body (in aikido - unarmed techniques)
tachi rei - bow in standing position
tanto - knife. In aikido the term refers to wooden knife.
tatami - mat, padded flooring
te gatana - "hand sword"
tera - temple (body part)
toma - big distance
tori - the one who is carrying out the technique, the thrower. Also see "shite"
tsugi ashi - sliding and follow up step. Tsugi ashi vs. ayumi ashi
tsuba - bokken's hand guard
tsuka - bokken's handle
tsuki - punch

Uchi - open hand strike
uchi deshi - live-in student, direct student of the sensei
uke - attacker, person being thrown. Also see "seme"
ukemi waza - the art of falling in response to a technique
ura - rear
ushiro - behind, backward

Waza - technique, method, group of techniques

Yame - stop
yoko - side
yokomen - side of the head
yondan - 4th degree black belt rank
yudansha - any black belt rank holder

Zanshin - lit. remaining mind; alerted state of mind right after performing technique(s)
zarei - bow in a seiza
zori - sandals
zubon - pants

Japanese Counting

ichi - one
ni - two
san - three
shi/yon - four
go - five
roku - six
shichi/nana - seven
hachi - eight
kyu - nine
ju - ten

Other books of interest. Available from Amazon.com and other book stores.

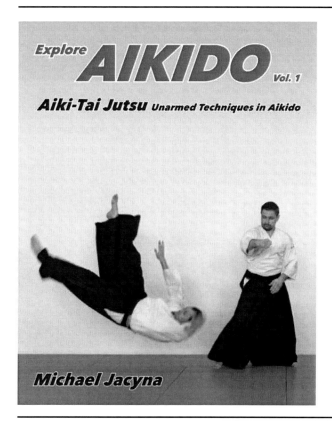

Explore AIKIDO Vol. 1
Aiki-Tai Jutsu
Unarmed Techniques in Aikido

The volume showcases wide range of unarmed aikido techniques including:

- Suwari Waza
- Hanmi Hantachi Waza
- Tachi Waza
- Futari Dori
- Randori
- Kaeshi Waza
- Ukemi

ISBN-13: 978-1948038003
ISBN-10: 1948038005

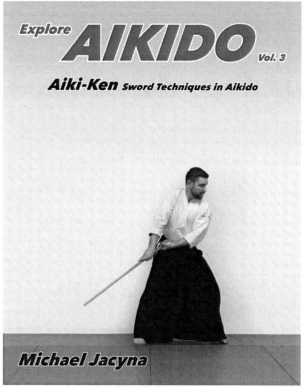

Explore AIKIDO Vol. 3
Aiki-Ken
Sword Techniques in Aikido

The volume showcases a wide range of sword techniques in aikido including:

- Aiki-Ken Etiquette
- Bokken Suburi
- Bokken Kihon/Kata
- Ken Nage
- Ken Dori
- Kumi Tachi

ISBN 13: 978-1948038027
ISBN 10: 1948038021